THE LABORATORY OF SILENCE

DR. ROBERT A. RUSSELL

Audio Enlightenment Press

Giving Voice to the Wisdom of the Ages

Printed in the United States of America

First Printing, 2022
ISBN 978-1-941489-90-1

www.RobertARussell.Org

Table of Contents

To W. J. A.

*Who gave his life
to serve.*

*"Greater love hath
no man than this,
that a man lay
down his life for
his friends."*

*His was the first
soul I had the
privilege of
meeting in the
Silence, and to that
glowing personality
who thought first
and always of
those dearer to
him than himself,
this book is
dedicated.*

— The Author.

FOREWORD

Spiritual growth, elevation to a higher plane of existence both here and hereafter, is the great object of life. By comparison with this supreme achievement, knowledge of and familiarity with metaphysical processes is of slight importance. But the mathematician must first learn thoroughly the elementary parts of that science before he may be accepted as an authority in the world of equations; the logician must master dialectics before he advances to discursive reasoning. So those who search for spiritual truth will find a formula useful, as necessary as a guidepost on a strange road or a beacon in the darkness.

THE LABORATORY OF SILENCE was selected as a title for this book because it indicates that only by sustained effort may those interested in spiritual progress hope to become proficient. I do not wish to be understood as taking the position that the method I have endeavored to describe is the only way in which the desired result may be achieved. Rather is it the way I have found to be most satisfactory. Other paths might be followed with equally happy effect.

"Seek and ye shall find," said the Great Teacher. The method set forth here is one which has been tried and not found wanting. That it may be used by many who will find by its aid that "peace which passeth understanding" is the earnest wish of

— The Author.

*"The Lord is in His
holy temple, let all
the earth keep silence
before Him."*

+

*"He that dwelleth
in the secret place
of the most High
shall abide under
the shadow of the
Almighty."*

+

*"Be silent, all flesh,
before Jehovah."*

The Laboratory of Silence

THE SILENCE is what the word implies, a place of stillness. It does not have a specific location, dimension or boundary, neither can it be measured or compassed. Psychologically speaking it is a state of mind, the simplest function of consciousness. Theologically speaking it is a form of prayer, the most subtle form known.

Belonging to the intangible world of Spirit, its phenomena is beyond the range of sense. It becomes real only to those who in a state of absolute mental and physical abstraction have withdrawn from the world to become the instruments of Spirit. Abstraction in this sense means passivity, not indolence; an utter abandonment of all physical and indiscriminate conscious activity. It is an unconfined state in which all labor is effortless. There is no illusion in Silence. Its law is the law of correspondence. The Silence responds to us as we respond to the Silence. In other words, the tone is determined by our pitch.

In one of his marvelous essays Emerson says: "The finite alone has wrought and suffered, the Infinite lies stretched in smiling repose." What a picture of God, eternally in repose, a selective attention in which to know is to be. This is egoism. It is the power of the Silence, the peace that passeth understanding; a poise so tranquil and serene that it no longer considers adverse conditions, opposing forces or confusion.

Many of us are like patchwork quilts I have seen — a little here and a little there. What we need is not more patches, but a reorganization of that we already have; a resolute effort to bring order out of chaos, and establish a response only to that which is good. Spiritual sight is intensified in Silence, but the law by which it operates is impersonal. It will create that which you perceive, whether it be good or evil, pleasant or unpleasant. The form will be always in accordance with your pattern, or your mental acceptance.

"Hold thy peace at the Presence of the Lord Jehovah; for the day of Jehovah is at hand." In this inner stillness you are actually standing in the Presence of God, the Father that doeth the works. He is in that place and you will in Spirit commune with Him. "See to it, then, that thyself is there, and the Supreme Being shall not be absent from the chamber where thou sittest." The only command is to "stand still," and see the Salvation which He will work for you. "The Lord shall fight for you, and ye shall hold your peace." The only condition imposed upon you is to "rest in the Lord," and wait patiently for Him. It matters not how great or how small your problem or difficulty. Possessing yourself in Silence, every stone shall be rolled away. No asking, no begging and no beseeching, for these are negative attitudes and imply doubt. Any form of struggling will delay your good. "Be still and know!" The battle is God's, and you have nothing to do with it. All flows out naturally when you are at one with your Source.

A NEW WORLD WILL BE YOURS

Centering yourself in this inner quiet, a new world will move in upon you. Things hitherto unknown will be revealed. Dilating your spiritual vision, carnality will be dissolved, and a wider sky will break upon your view. In fact, it is the only state in which there is absolute liberation. No longer contemplating sickness, fear, disease and lack, you will be suffused with the vital Power of the Central Life. As a partaker of the Divine Nature you will share His Vibrations. For a time it may seem as though you were going to leave your body. This is an experience which has frightened many. Do not be alarmed; whatsoever is rooted in God cannot be plucked up. Abiding in Christ, you are courageous and fearless. Established in Him, He will not suffer your feet to be moved. Metaphysicians explain this phenomenon or sensation differently, but I am convinced that it is a growing pain, attendant upon re-birth, the mergence of the old with the new. Then at other times you may be suffused in light, sometimes blue, sometimes yellow, and occasionally white. The last is the ideal of the meditative life because it is a composite of all the others, a symbol of Oneness. It is sometimes called the white Light of Spirit. But this is not all, for leading up to the light stage in your unfoldment, the inner imagery may include many things. Sometimes a great exaltation, a glorious feeling of freedom, the sensation of flying in space, inspiring ideas, sounds, symbols, pictures, and even delicate and delightful odors may be perceptible to you. In the Silence, this or any similar phenomena is of the Holy Spirit, and denotes a profound stillness, within and without. You are comprehending God by taking on the Divine Nature.

ENERGY EQUAL TO ANY DEMAND

"They that wait upon the Lord shall renew their strength; they shall mount up with wings as eagles; they shall run, and not be weary; they shall walk, and not faint." This statement of Isaiah is as applicable to our bodies as to our minds. "Nature never runs on a narrow margin." Stored up in the countless millions of cells in your body there are tons of energy which may be released at will. This has been proved many times by what Professor James called "second wind." But we do not stop there, for scientists are now proving that there is a third, a fourth, a fifth and a sixth level of energy or physical reserve equal to any demand. "Waiting upon the Lord" in Silence is the secret of release of this Infinite Power. To possess the Universal Wholeness from which you came, you must be conscious of it at your center.

The process of priming your submerged center in stillness is similar to the practice of astronomers who dig deep wells near their observatories. The one on Mount Wilson, in California, is four hundred feet in depth. From Copernicus down, searchers of interplanetary space have dug these wells that by going into them they might see further into the skies. These astronomers, figuratively speaking, go down into their mental selves in order to hurl their minds out farther into the celestial universe beyond. Thus the deeper you go, that is, the more profound your silence becomes, the more of reality you will perceive.

Now as it becomes apparent that you are actually touching the Hem of His Garment, you will know that there is no problem to solve, no disease to heal and nothing for you to do. "All that the Father hath is already yours." Your function is simply to accept that which is already there. Know this: The Allness of God is manifested through you, and not by you. The whole responsibility is God's but if you are going to receive you must take that which is so freely given. And since you are in no way involved in the materialization of any desire, you must be still enough and trustful enough to let God demonstrate Himself.

This phase of the work may be new to you, but it is one of the most important steps in your development. Many make the mistake of dwelling on sickness, error, and problems in the Silence. But when you do this, you separate yourself from the Good. You cease to be a channel for the Divine. Nothing ever came from nothing but nothing. Nothing ever came from disease but disease. Everything after its kind.

DON'T TAKE PROBLEMS INTO SILENCE

Suppose, for instance, that you are vexed by some problem, and you take it into the Silence for solution. Can it be done? No! most assuredly No! The more you fix your attention upon a problem, especially in the Silence, the more real it becomes. To discover its cause is to make it worse. "Ye shall know the Truth," says the Master, "and the Truth shall make you free." The truth about what? Your problem? No! The Truth about God. As long as you work with sense you are contemplating, and reflecting, illusion, for you are working in the mental realm and not the Spiritual. The words of God are "Yea" and "Amen," "which signifies that for God to know is to be." On the plane of Truth you must speak the language of Truth. Universal Mind comprehends only Truth.

Then, too, as I shall point out later on, you must keep your vision pointed and clear. Recall the story of the cat that went up to London to see the queen. How thrilled we were anticipating its return—at the prospect of hearing at first hand what happened in court—the banquet, the gowns, the music, etc. Then the disappointment, the chagrin, to learn that all it saw was a mouse! The cat you see had a mouse consciousness. It was more interested in the rodent that it was in the queen. This is true also of you. If you are more interested In error, limitation, problems "loaves and fishes," or your body than you are in Heaven Consciousness, then you will miss God. "Seek ye first the Kingdom of God and His righteousness, and all these things shall be added unto you."

To summarize, then, you do not enter the Silence to know the Truth about a problem or a disease, but rather the Truth about God, that which eternally is. God is Light, and where Light is there is no darkness. "Let your Light so shine before men and so glorify the Father of Light in Whom is no variableness, no shadow made by turning." Darkness is not in itself an entity, but only absence of light. And the more light you obtain the less darkness you will have. The same hypothesis is true also of disease. What we call sickness is merely absence of health, and not a thing of itself. Turn on the Light and you see its nothingness!

Health peace and prosperity are effects and not causes. The great conflict which divides your good is in the intellectual mind and not the Spiritual (superconscious) mind. Representing as they do, the two extremities of mentation, the negative and positive poles of the mental body, they are both necessary, but there must be a reversal of polarity before the I AM can come into Its own. Perfect cause is inherent in each of us, but it must be unified with the Whole. There must be an inward transformation before there can be an outward manifestation. "Every atom in the universe can act on every other atom, but only through the atom next to it." To affect your body then you must vision through the mind which is next to God, that which senses perfect being and produces perfect results. There are only two sides to Truth, the inside and the outside. One is darkness (intellectual mind), and the other is Light (intuitional mind). This is vividly portrayed on Calvary. On the other side of the cross of Christ was darkness and death, but on this side is Light and Life.

TO KNOW SPIRIT IS TO BE ONE WITH IT

To have the Kingdom of Heaven is to drop self—to become the willing instrument of Spirit. "It is not I," said Jesus, "but the Father within Me that doeth the works." The external conditions in your life correspond exactly to the internal conditions. What you see is but a reflection of what you have conceived. If you have conceived the opposite of truth in your consciousness, you have materialized that opposite in your body or your affairs. To know Spirit you must become one with Spirit. You must be identified with Truth before you can receive truth. Even as the sunlight streaming through a burning glass will dissolve snow, the white Light of Spirit streaming through your consciousness will dissolve falsity and error. "Neither shall they say, 'Lo here!' or 'lo there!' for behold the Kingdom of God (Light) is within you."

"Let your Light so shine before men that they may see your good works and glorify your Father which is in Heaven." For some obscure reason many in the church have interpreted this command to pertain to money, and even now we may hear it used as an offertory sentence before the collection. To me it is a misuse of Scripture, for it means something infinitely greater than nickels and dimes—something far more important. The Light referred to is Spirit, or Life, and means the Third Person of the Trinity. God is Light and they who worship Him must worship Him in Light or God Consciousness. It is the Spirit that giveth life, therefore we must lay hold of Spirit. This is the Power within you, the same power that resurrected Jesus Christ from the dead and overcomes all physical ailments. Ask any physician what causes sickness and disease, and he will answer it is due to lowered vitality, or congestion. This, of course, means a lack of Life or Light. We all need this quickening of Spirit, but the question which confronts us is, how shall we get it?

LIFE AND HEALTH FROM WITHIN

Know this: There is no life in medicine or nostrums of any kind, for it cannot be added from the outside. Permanent Life and health is always evolved from within, and cannot come from any other source. You must make connection with the Universal Life current through your mind. Think Life, talk Life, breathe Life, pray Life, sing Life, feel Life, and you will be filled with Life. This is the meaning of letting "your Light shine." Jesus came "that ye might have Life more abundantly." Thus when you are filled with this abundant, buoyant Life, you will be glorifying the Father who dwelleth in you. Yes, you will be able to do the things Jesus did. Believing in and using this Life you will never die, and having this Life you will radiate health, peace and prosperity.

The first step, then, is to know that you are an individualization of the Omnipresent Life of Spirit, and that when you become one with your Source, this life is set free to manifest its Good. God Life permeates everything and is inhibited only by our thoughts. If they are centered in the Life idea we express life. If they are centered in the body or words which are not in accord with the Life idea, we express decay. The flow has been shut off, and there is congestion. "He that will, let him take the Water of Life freely."

In a very real sense, then, you and I are "Children of Light." We are living prisms designed especially to reveal the nature of Light, to show forth the purifying and cleansing power of Spirit; in other words, to let the Universal Wholeness take possession of our corporate natures and shine through them with a radiance that makes them glorious, harmonious and peaceful. This cannot be done, however, unless the Light is allowed to shine through us. Go into Westminster Abbey in the evening and its stained glass windows are dead, but enter that sacred shrine in the morning, when the sun is streaming through those thousands of tiny bits of glass, and they are gorgeous to behold. We have a striking illustration in the Life of St. Paul. As Saul of Tarsus he was potentially a great man, yet dead. Then on the highway to Damascus he was filled with Light. It shone through him and his greatness was revealed in a surprising manner. In the first instance he was hiding his Light under a bushel. In the second instance he became one with the Divine order, and his entire consciousness was illumined and glorified, revealing that which had hitherto been hidden.

WILLIAM DUDLEY PELLEY'S EXPERIENCE

Coming down to contemporary history we have another striking illustration in the life of William Dudley Pelley. The story is set forth dramatically in his brochure, "Seven Minutes in Eternity." It was unquestionably an experience in the Silence, and happened one night in his home near Pasadena, California. Says Mr. Pelley:

> I brought something back with me from that Ecstatic Interlude, which suddenly began to function in strange powers of perception. I went about my bungalow in the days that followed as if I were still in a sort of trance, which verily I was. And then came experience number two, not quite so theatric and therefore harder to describe. One night, while still imbued with the "feeling" of my fourth-dimensional adventure, I took down a volume of Emerson and opened it by chance at his essay on the Over-Soul. In the middle of it, though not reading any specific line, I had a queer moment of confusion, a sort of cerebral vertigo, then a strange physical sensation at the very top of my head as if a beam of pure white light had poured down from above and bored n shaft straight into my skull. In

that instant a vast weight went out of my whole physical ensemble. A veil was torn away.

I saw no "vision," but something had happened and was continuing to happen. A cascade of pure, cool, wonderful peace was falling down from somewhere above me and cleansing me. My book fell from my fingers to the rug and stayed there. I sat there staring into space. I was not the same man I had been a moment before! I mean this physically, mentally, spiritually. I knew somehow that I had acquired senses and perceptions that I could never hope to describe to any second person, and yet they were as real to me as the shape of my wrists.

My first dramatic physical reaction was a sudden change in the components of my body. And the change soon began to manifest itself in concrete form. One day in my office I took a package of cigarettes from my desk. About to apply a light to one of them, I heard a voice say as gently as any worried mother might caution a careless son, "Oh Bill, give up your cigarettes!" And even before it occurred to me that no one was present in the flesh to address me thus audibly, I answered: "All right!" and tossed the package into the nearby waste basket. I went all that day without smoking. Next morning again, I reached for my tobacco tin across my desk to load up my corncob. It was knocked from my hands with a slap that tossed it in the air and deposited it bottom upward at my feet with the tobacco spilled out. No cautioning this time. But I knew!

I haven't smoked tobacco in any form from that day to the present. Moreover I haven't had the slightest ill effect nor did I go through the agonizing torture of "breaking off!" I just didn't smoke any more — didn't have the nervous urge — didn't even give tobacco a thought. The same strange prohibition seemed to shut down on coffee, tea, alcohol and meats. I endured not the slightest distress in giving these items up. They simply ceased to exist for me. And, inversely, a strange new sensation began to manifest itself in my muscles and organs. I had the glorious feeling of physical detachment from the handicaps of bodily matter. No form of bodily exercise seemed to take energy that I bad consciously to supply. I bad always been slightly stoop-shouldered. Without any unusual exercise my spine straightened of itself, so to speak.

Mr. Pelley states that he no longer experiences insomnia, and that his understanding has been growing in clarity every day and hour since that epochal night. "What is this thing which happened to me, and why did it happen?" he asks. "First, I believe my subconscious hunger after what the Bible terms 'the things of the spirit' — that is, the sincere desire to penetrate behind the mediocrity of three-meals-a-day living and ascertain what mystery lies behind the Golgotha of existence — attracted to me spiritual forces of a very high and altruistic order, which aided me in making a hyper-dimensional visitation. I believe such hunger will always attract such forces."

LIGHT OF THE WORLD IS FOR ALL

"Ye are the Light of the world," said Jesus, and to be inoculated with this Light is the greatest experience that can come to any person. It cannot be purchased in bottles or from teachers. It must be earned, and earned with a price. For most of us it will mean hours, weeks, yea, even months of seeking and unfolding, but every time we turn inward to God we are like the flowers in the spring turning our faces toward the light. Then when God shines through the Soul, we see the Light we are seeking does not have to be snatched from some cosmic shelf or added from the outside, but is already there, waiting our appropriation.

One night quite late I had occasion to go to a church for some vestments. Finding the key I entered the building. Everything was strange and incomprehensible, and nothing but darkness was apparent to me. Then I found the switch and turned on the light. Illumined by electrical current much was immediately revealed—pews, an altar, an organ, candlesticks and many other things. An instant before none of these was perceptible to me, so now I ask: Who put them there? Was it the light? No, the light but revealed that which had been there all the time. Then where did the darkness go? It did not go anywhere, for there was nothing to go. Darkness is merely absence of light and has no existence except that which is occasioned by absence of the positive quality, light. The finite perceives darkness and the Infinite perceives Light. Jesus came that the darkness might be dispelled. As far as you are concerned, your concept of darkness and its permanence is all there is to darkness. This is true also of evil, sickness, death, and lack. They exist only in your mind and have no counterpart in spirit. Glowing always in abundance, the spirit manifests all that God has created. This alone is permanent and worth while, and nothing else matters.

THE LAW OF THE LORD IS PERFECT

"In the beginning was the Word, and the Word was with God, and the Word was God. The same was in the beginning with God. All things were made by Him, and without Him was not anything made that was made." "The Law of the Lord is perfect," therefore that which He created is indestructible, permanent and true. Anything that God did not create has no reality or permanence. If you do not believe this, try to mix the perfect with the imperfect—light and darkness, evil and good, life and death, sickness and health, harmony and discord, happiness and sorrow, hate and love. Like oil and water, they will not mix. Only that which is enduring can be mixed—that which proceeds from God. Anything which He did not make has not been made and is nothing at all. Now take those qualities which were created, put them together and you have the essence of divinity. Light, Good, Life, Health, Harmony, Happiness and Love—each one reflects the glory of the others. All of which proves that. negation is illusion and false sense. "It is the false sense that needs education," and not the Spirit.

What I have here said is analogous to our dream states, in which some of the most tragic experiences have been enacted. In your dream it may seem as though your house is on fire and you are being burned, or that you are falling out of the window of a high building. It may be you struggled or fought to save yourself from such a horrible fate, but these were only visions in your mind and did not really happen. When you came to your senses the vision vanished, and no longer troubled you. After all, you were not really in your dream. The man on the bed was the victim of illusion, and his struggle was futile. Jesus said, "I came not to destroy but to fulfill." Stop fighting and struggling with your concepts of

13

evil. After all, you cannot free yourself from anything, nor can you win over anything you fight. Rather let Spirit fulfill Himself in you and reveal that which is perfect and good. Be conscious even in your waking state that there is only one Power, and one reality. Evil will cease to exist only when you cease to believe in it.

"Arise, shine, for thy Light is come and the glory of the Lord is risen upon thee." "Acquaint now thyself with Him and be at peace; thereby Good shall come unto thee." Illumined by this Light which lights everyone that comes into the world, there is nothing else to understand. But to get out of sickness and poverty you must lift your consciousness above the darkness. "The Light shineth in darkness, and the darkness comprehendeth it not." No matter how dark your mind or affairs may be, God is there in the fullness of His glory waiting to deliver you, as Jesus was asleep in the boat during the storm on Galilee, awaiting the call of His disciples in their need. "God is omnipresent," everywhere existent, but a darkened consciousness cannot comprehend Him. To be in you He must be in your consciousness. It was never intended that you should be in bondage or distress. Purify your beliefs and you can make your world just what you wish it to be.

RELIGION AND HEALTH SYNONYMOUS

The Bible says, "God is too pure to behold iniquity. Therefore, as the Bible states, He does not see both good and evil. He sees only Good, that which is whole, and to be whole is to be complete. "Be ye holy, even as I am holy." Interpreting this command metaphysically we should say: "Be ye whole, even as I am whole," or, "Be ye well, even as I am well." Religion and health are synonymous, and cannot be separated. The word "holy" is a cognate form of the English word "heal." Other words coming from the same root are healthy, hale and wholly. The same thought is also conveyed in that other English word "well." From this we get weal, wealth, and wealthy. Interpreting the word literally, well means wealth, not only in purse, but in body, in mind and in spirit. The etymology of the Latin word "salus" is also illuminating. The cognate forms of "salus" are salvation, salve, save and Savior. A Savior is a Life or Health giver. Thus we say in the Nicean creed: "I believe in the Holy Ghost, the Lord and Giver of Life." The Holy Ghost might be interpreted as the Giver of that which is Whole or well. In reality, He is the materializing Force of the whole of Life. And when I say the whole of Life, I mean everything which is necessary to perfect expression. If your pocketbook is sick or your body is ailing, then you are not whole. Maybe you have been trying to look in two directions at once, beholding both good and evil, which is equivalent to setting up a battlefield in consciousness.

God is indivisible and complete. He is unhurtable and eternal, the one and only value, and since it is a law of mind that it always sees and reflects what it looks for, it behooves us to persistently look for that which is perfect or Godlike. As long as you see disease you will fight disease, thus creating a dead spot in consciousness. And this is true of all things undesirable. On the other hand, when you have the health or Life consciousness you will express prosperity in every department of your Being. "Whatever you fight always fights back," and the last stage of a fight is always worse than the first. There is only One Mind, One Principle, One Substance and One Law in the entire Universe. Anything less than the One is imperfect and incomplete. And the One never fights or struggles.

WORK ONLY IN REALM OF POSITIVE

Stop trying to work with opposites, good and evil, light and darkness, health and sickness, silence and noise, heat and cold. The negative is never anything but absence of the positive. All you need do is supply the positive and the negative disappears.

Suppose, for instance, that the fire in your house had gone out. It is a cold, wintery day and you are freezing. What must you do to get warm? Well, the imprudent or ignorant man might work with both heat and cold, but the wise man would use only heat. He would light a fire and the cold would disappear.

The same analogy is applicable to your body as well. All that is necessary for the annihilation of disease is to turn on the light. No longer in bondage to material laws you will simply drop from your mind (through non-recognition) any image of disease or lack and the evil will drop out of your world. There is positively nothing that can remain in your body or affairs unless there is a matrix (thought form) to hold it. By that I mean a consciousness which corresponds to it. The affirmative factor in all disease is consciousness, and the only support which it has. Thus a person troubled with rheumatism has a rheumatic consciousness, a person with cancer has a cancer consciousness, and so on. The same thing is true of sorrow, which also is a mental disease. Grief is self-created and cannot touch you except through your own mind. It must depart by the same route over which it came. Its antidote is the true concept of life, which makes you incapable of tears. "Better a smile for the living than fountains of tears for the so-called dead." What is past help is past sorrow. The one sure way to make those who have passed from this plane unhappy and miserable is to weep and agonize over them. When you are one with life you will rejoice in the passing of your dear ones, knowing that life has no cessation or separation. You will know that transition from one plane to another is but the passage from life abundant to life more abundant, and that your loved ones are more vividly alive in that state than they were here.

LET GO OF THAT WHICH IS IMPERFECT

"Repent ye, for the Kingdom of Heaven is at hand." Repentance means to "turn away from," to let go of that which is less than perfect. The moment you turn away from sin or evil, that moment you are forgiven and healed, and not before. The affirmative factor in healing or release is the metaphysical process of turning away, or dropping from your mind that which you do not want.

Life in the Silence is one perfect, harmonious whole. And you cannot draw nigh this place without feeling a new sense of regnancy, a new sense of completeness and a new power such as you never before had. All tension is released, fears are banished, sickness flees, and the personal man becomes impersonal, triumphant and free. What a privilege to practice the Presence of God, to turn on the "Great Eternal Light," to bless, to heal and to renew. Merging the old self with the New Self is like throwing a bucket of dirty water into the Atlantic ocean. In the vastness of the virgin deep, the dirt is lost to sight completely and the waters become one. Illumined by this Light you are standing in a place, a place more real than the house in which you live. This place I shall designate as yourself, not the fractional self, limited and incomplete, but your Greater Self, the I AM of God!

Jesus said: "Ye must be born again." But where and how? In the alembic of your soul (Light Center), by the perception of Truth. But what is this new birth and how does it come? It is the mergence of your little everyday personality with the Greater Personality which is God. And it is accomplished through meditation and contemplation in the Silence. This fundamental state of consciousness then, is the distributing Center of God, and the mind is the operator receiving what it sends. Literally, it is the scientific process of "casting your bread upon the waters" or ethers. Working according to Law, and meeting the conditions, you cannot fail. That which you send out (affirm) comes back to you. Being a representative of Spirit, God is within you, the universe is back of you, and whatsoever you do shall prosper. Working in the Central Life you command the ether the world, the flesh and the devil, for all things are put under your feet. Yes, you can even speak the word (right idea) and your friend shall be healed. Words spoken in the Silence are your spiritual fiat. They are words of authority, accomplishing that whereunto they are sent.

DIRECT PATH TO UNIVERSAL SUPPLY

Never plead in the Silence, never struggle and never hope! Simply affirm (command) — be still — and know! Then with each recurring demonstration allow your consciousness to expand. This mode of prayer is dynamic and not static. It is the direct path to Universal Supply. It is not dangerous and is in no sense the manipulation of spirits, neither is it new. Its processes have been known and used by the seekers of every age. It was Carlyle who wrote: "Silence is the element in which great things fashion themselves together, that at length they may emerge, full-formed and majestic, into the daylight of life, which they are thenceforth to rule."

For the sake of emphasis, let me say again that you do not treat sickness in the Silence. You treat yourself and the sickness disappears. Its action is catalytic, having the properties to induce change, itself remaining unchanged. The Holy Spirit is the Great Catalyzer which takes rebellious cells and chemicalizes them into one harmonious whole. The same idea is conveyed in The Sacrament of Holy Communion. "The Body of our Lord Jesus Christ which was given for thee, preserve thy body and soul unto everlasting Life." "I pray God your whole Spirit and soul and body be preserved blameless."

Man is a tripartite being, and he must not ignore the body. It is by far the most wonderful of God's creations, and since we are to manifest through it we must keep it in repair. It must be a unit of divine action if it is to be charged with spirit. This is made plain by Paul in one of his Corinthian letters: "For as the body is one, and hath many members, and all the members of that one body, being many, are one body: so also is Christ. . . . For the body is not one member, but many. If the foot shall say, because I am not the hand, I am not of the body; is it therefore not of the body? And if the ear shall say, because I am not the eye, I am not of the body; is it therefore not of the body? If the whole body were an eye, where were the hearing? If the whole body were hearing, where were the smelling? But now hath God set the members every one of them in one body, as it hath pleased Him. But if they were all one member, where were the body? But now are they many members, yet but one body."

DOMINATE BODY BY LIGHT OF SOUL

Man, someone has said, is "a soul possessing a body." Thus, if your body is to be a vehicle for healing, it must be dominated by the Light of the Soul. It must be undefiled and blameless before God can use it to involve or evolve health. The most prolific sources of defilement, remember, are your words and your thoughts. The soul is so sensitive that a single unclean or unworthy thought is sufficient to abort the whole process.

Many persons squander much of their vital energy through discordant and uncontrolled thought. That which is indispensable to an equable state of health and beyond price is wasted. Later the body rises up in condemnation and we wonder why. This waste, which is due to a lack of poise, is continuous, and must be controlled, stopped, before health can be established. Through the inner life we must bring the outer life into Silence, combining high action with deep power. Since the power of the subjective (soul) mind is unlimited and inexhaustible, a perfect silence consists of your ability to effect a union between that and objective consciousness. The former is the generator or dynamo, and the latter is the motor turning the wheels. Concentrated power is dynamic, while unconcentrated power is static. The Great Within has everything you need, but it must be pressed into consciousness before it can be acted upon. When there is a free flow of concentrated power from within, you can accomplish anything you desire.

SILENCE IS SECRET PLACE OF POWER

Through practice of the Silence we learn not only to "receive fully and to use fully," but also how to conserve our power, keeping the body full of vital energy, which action not only prevents disease but maintains health. The Silence then is the Secret Place of Power, a device of Providence making the invisible visible and opening the windows of Heaven. Its action is noiseless because it is Infinite. Like the power that moves the world, it is soundless sound. Emerson speaks of it as "the extension of man on all sides into nature till his hands touch the stars, his eyes see through the earth, his ears understand the language of beast and bird, and heaven and earth talk with him." And again he says: "Silence is a solvent that destroys personality, and gives us leave to be great and Universal." I like this last statement of the eminent advocate of Unity, for we all want to be great, and the ultimate of every Christian is to be Universal.

As the wingless parasite (aphis) which thrives on rose bushes will, after the plant is dead, develop wings and migrate to living plants, so man, exhausting himself on the husks of the natural or worldly life, may retreat to his Central Self, there to develop the wings of the soul which will lift him above every obstacle, calamity and disease.

When little Palestine was facing inevitable end between two powerful enemies, debating frantically whether to cast her lot with Assyria or Egypt, Isaiah stepped into the picture and with characteristic firmness said: "With neither; in calmly resting your safety lieth, in quiet trust shall be your strength." And it was even as he said. However obstinate or impossible to ourselves, marvelous are the demonstrations when left to God. Trusting in Him, victory is assured from the beginning.

Another demonstration through this same law is found in the life of Jehoshaphat, king of Judah. During the onslaught of the Ammonites and the Moabites he, together with his people, turned in desperation to God for help, saying: "We have no might against this great multitude that cometh against us, neither know we what to do; but our eyes are upon Thee." Then the Spirit of the Lord came upon Jahaziel, and he said: "Hearken ye, all Judah; thus saith the Lord unto you: Be not afraid or dismayed by reason of this great multitude; for the battle is not yours, but God's. O Judah, fear not; but tomorrow go out against them, for the Lord will be with you. Ye shall not need to fight in this battle; set yourselves, stand ye still, and see the Salvation of the Lord with you."

CONFIDENT KNOWING BRINGS FRUITION

Know this: Your supply is always where your need is but like the Palestinians and others who have succeeded, you must claim it in quiet and silent trust. Of yourself you cannot heal, nor demonstrate anything. Be still and let God work through you. No matter how the storms may rage or how sore put you may be your chief business is to stand still. I care not how pressing or how urgent your need may be, what pressure you may be under all the struggling, all the fretting, all the worry and all the beseeching will do you not one bit of good. The language of Deity is the language of confidence. It is the confident knowing that brings the manifestation, and not the much struggling with words. The only enemy with which you have to contend is in your own household, the false belief in an external power which is greater than the power within you.

How are you going to meet this resistance? Are you going to fight it? No, that would spell defeat. Rather you will look upon it as the aviator looks upon the air in front of his propeller. You will use it to sustain you. To resist anything is to weaken yourself and your energies. Especially is this true of jealousy, antagonism, envy and criticism. Every time you recognize evil in any form, or engage in or struggle with negative emotions or attitudes, you are transferring a portion of your life force to the object or person that incited you. Thus he becomes the beneficiary of the most priceless thing you have; he gets the benefit, and you are the loser. This thought was implied in the Scriptures: It is harder for a rich man to enter the Kingdom of Heaven than for a camel to go through the eye of a needle. The rich man expends or transfers so much of his vital energy on the things he possesses that they become the whole of his life. "Thou foolish one," Jesus said to the rich husbandman, "this night is thy soul required of thee; and the things which thou hast prepared, whose shall they be?" The Sermon on the Mount also stresses the futility of things. "Lay not up for yourselves treasure upon the earth, where moth and rust consume." Things must have a measure of care; therefore the less you have the greater will be your freedom. The only things which have a rightful place in your life are those which help you to express life better. They need not be many nor expensive. What you make of what you have determines their power. The greatest values are spiritual and not material, which accounts for Jesus' question: "For what shall it profit a man if he gain the whole world and lose his own soul?"

LIFT YOURSELF ABOVE PERSONALITIES

To ascend you must have momentum, a momentum born of stillness. It would be far better for you to meet innuendo and strife with an inward smile, saying to yourself each time any unpleasant thing comes upon you: "I must be about my Father's business." Deny the hurt as you would an unwelcome caller at your door. Consecrating yourself to the Will of the Father lifts you above the limitation of personalities and makes you impersonal. "Thou wilt keep him in perfect peace whose mind is stayed on Thee."

"Because thou hast made the Lord which is my refuge . . . even the Most High . . . thy habitation, there shall no evil befall thee, neither shall any plague come nigh thy dwelling. For He shall give His angels charge over thee to keep thee in all thy ways." This is the best bond in all the world. It is drawn on the Bank of Heaven and sealed by the King. His signature is upon it and the Universal Mind is back of it. All you need to cash this bond is the same faith which you have in a hundred-dollar bill with the seal of the United States upon it. Take it into the Silence and see what it will buy. It has the greatest purchasing power in the world; take it into the Silence and see what it will buy!

Having now realized that spiritual cargo comes over silent seas, and that God does His greatest work in this "fundamental state of mind," you will readily see the importance of Jesus' injunction: "When thou prayest, enter into thine inner chamber (Silence), and having shut the door (mortal mind), pray to thy Father which is in secret, and thy Father which seeth in secret shall reward thee openly."

Working in the Laboratory of Silence is the act of taking possession of your mental and spiritual world. It is an attitude toward the whole of life, "praying without ceasing," letting every action of your life be done in poise. All the energy of the body must be employed and conserved without any conscious direction. Thus every work or activity will be approached with serenity and poise, that we may become magnets of power. "Praying without ceasing" means an hourly cultivation and practice of the inner and outer stillness which overcomes restlessness and waste. "You shall receive power," said Jesus, "when the Holy Spirit is come upon you." The Holy Spirit is the catalytic force of God in man. He is God in action, and the only activity which generates power. Thus to live in Him is to have the majesty and power of calmness. Jesus understood this secret, which accounts for His dominion over everything. All He needed to do was to speak the Word and the results were instantaneous. He changed water into wine, raised the dead, healed the sick and cast out demons. Those who touched His body felt the vivifying shock of this inward Presence and their needs were immediately met. God, however, will not do anything for you except that which He can do through you. Every demonstration rests finally with yourself and your consciousness. This is the channel through which the Holy Spirit works, and it must be kept open and free. To be in tune with Spirit is to be in touch with the fullness of God; no more lassitude, exhaustion or fatigue. Living, working and thinking incessantly in the Great Eternal Calm, you will be drawing upon the inexhaustible reservoir of omnipresent energy and Intelligence. Concentrated vitality will flow into the natural man, establishing a balance between wear and repair.

PUT WHOLE BEING INTO PRAYER

The Silence is, of course, but a form of prayer. There are many other forms as effective, depending on the Spirit which you put into them. The Hopi snake dance, for instance, is one of the most dynamic of Indian prayers, and according to observers has never failed to bring rain. To that bromidic individual known as the "man in the street" it is an enigma, but to the metaphysician it is an open book. The Indian succeeds because he puts his whole being into his prayer, body, mind, and Spirit. He concentrates every energy on the fulfillment of his desire. Most of us fail because we never get beyond the forms. Prayer to us is an intellectual function, a mere mouthing of phrases, and seldom gets beyond the mind. "Stir up the Gift" means to emote (motion within). Put yourself into any prayer you make. Fill it with emotion and, like the well-aimed arrow from the bow, it will go straight to its destination. It is the difference between the average radio station broadcasting its vibrations in every direction, and the trans-Atlantic station concentrating its power in the Marconi beam. Prayer rightly made will vibrate the ethers and penetrate to the very Throne of God.

Prayer is creative only when coupled with feeling from the emotional center. Prayer must be made alive by constructive emotion, or shaking up within, otherwise it is dead. Fill your prayers, then, with life. Live in the success of them before they are answered. Offer your deepest gratitude and thankfulness. Breathe into them the Breath of Life and they will come to life. To pray aright, then, is first to express thankfulness and gratitude for blessings already received, to covet for everybody what you are asking for yourself. When you are truly thankful, you involuntarily take a deep breath. You inspire, which means put life into or make alive. Spirit vibrates more perfectly in a thankful heart or state of mind than in one that is unthankful. Prayers are lifeless unless there is thankfulness, enthusiasm and gratitude. First the emotion, constructive agitation within, the mental picture, and then the fulfillment.

SELECT A FORM WHICH FITS YOU

After all, it does not matter what form or method you use. The important thing is to select the one that is most natural to you, the one which will bring you into most intimate relationship with God. People go to California by different routes. Some go by the comfortable trans-continental trains, and less fortunate ones by bus. They all arrive, but the man who goes by air takes the direct and rapid route, reaching his destination more quickly. I am offering the Silence to you because I am air-minded, and because I have through experience found it is the most direct and satisfactory route. As I said in the beginning, it is without form, and is impersonal. You can talk in the Silence, but the Silence does not talk. It has no independent quality of its own. The process of entering this place is a process of losing yourself that you may find the Greater Self. The real purpose is to "seek first the Kingdom of Heaven." It is a period of gestation, evolving from yourself that which you are to become. As someone has said: "It can be likened to the life within the stalk, concentrating as it were upon the building and forming of the bud, pushing out, expanding, swelling itself, becoming big with that which is unfolding, evolving from itself."

Having found this place, the I AM consciousness will be in full command of all your forces, guiding you into the paths of Truth and Light, and you are now ready to release your power, the I AM in you. This "I" of Spirit is the only one in existence. Just as there is but one you, one One, and one "I," so there is only one God. Thus, working in the impersonal "I" consciousness, you have the resources of the Universe at your command, to do with as you please. When you declare I AM, you are using the most sacred and dynamic word you may utter; and because of this, you will henceforth judge righteously. Never again will you say: "I AM sick," or "I AM poor." Such assertions are false. The I AM of you is never sick and never poor. It is the personal man that is sick or poor, but never the "I." Be obedient to the law and you will beget good; be disobedient and you will beget evil.

SECRET OF THE ABOUNDING LIFE

Thoughts (words) are causative and the mind is like a burning glass. Use it positively and it magnifies and makes plain. Use it negatively and it blisters or burns. The I AM of Jesus was magnified to such an extent that He could compel results in everything. Like a great wireless station He could broadcast its power to distant points and persons. "I and the Father are One," Jesus said, and this knowledge was the secret of the abounding life which He imparted to all those in need. When you are One with the Father, you too will become a distributing center of Spirit, able to impart this abounding life to others.

Now, before we proceed with our study, let us be guided by Jesus' formula: "But thou, when thou prayest, enter into thine inner chamber, and having shut thy door, pray to thy Father which is in secret." Too much emphasis cannot be placed upon the matter of shutting the door. This refers to the outer or objective mind, that phase of your life so peculiarly related to sense and the ordinary things of existence. In an age when bitter disputes about beliefs were common, and it was not unusual for men to sacrifice their lives rather than their opinions, Donne set down in his diary the extraordinary difficulty with which he prayed even in secret. Donne was a devout man, but he complains that a buzzing insect, a fly crawling on the window pane, served to distract him and make of no effect the petitions he poured out to God.

Without doubt, the objective mind is the greatest obstacle to those seeking an absolute state of abstraction, reporting as it may some two hundred ideas every minute. To many it is an increasing distraction, becoming more active as the effort to enter the Silence becomes more persistent. But mental chaos is turning into everything and getting nothing. It is like taking a bucketful of water to a well. You must be empty before you can receive. Recognize that the Silence is a cosmos and not chaos. It is peace and not confusion. The first is strength and the second is weakness.

Know this: Objective life cannot intrude upon the subjective when attention is specific. When the attention is allowed to wander, "we receive not, because we are asking amiss." "He that ruleth his spirit (attention) is greater than he that taketh a city." All inward opening is through the attention. "Behold I stand at the door and knock: if any man hear My voice, and open the door, I will come in to him, and will sup with him." It is true that "desire in the heart is God tapping at the door of our consciousness with His Infinite supply," but if we have not opened the door which connects the soul with the mind, we cannot find the words which are health to all our flesh.

But how slow down this undesirable action of mind? By concentration and focalization. You are going to be positive and unwavering. You are going to tune in to one thing at a time, and hold all conflicting thoughts in abeyance, without effort, labor, or tenseness. The body, mind and spirit must work in unity, not as separate bodies, but as one. Just as you have to. learn the rules of bridge or any other game, just as you have to train the faculties in the mastery of any accomplishment, so you have to train the mind before you can realize the totality of God.

PROFICIENCY IN CONCENTRATION

Concentration is but attention at white heat. It is the ability to keep the mind under control, to direct it in one direction. And, since life is change, there will be fluctuations in focus.

Consciousness moves at a rapid rate, and as man may contend with as many as two hundred different ideas or thoughts a minute, he cannot at first long attend to any one of them. This should be no cause for discouragement, however, but rather an incentive to higher achievement. Concentration is like a game, and might be called the game of unity, harmonizing through elimination the finer forces of our being. To the man who enters into it seriously, there is no defeat. He finds it fascinating. What if the attention does wander, if the mental gaze shifts? This is no obstacle, for the object is to exclude all but the unifying idea which he has set as his goal. He will bring his attention back a hundred times if need be, for he knows there is no progress without concentration.

Here, then, are some "does" and "don'ts" in the mastery of concentration:

Do not force concentration; that is, do not hold the mind.

Do not resist vagrant thoughts.

Do not hold more than one idea at a time.

Do not attend to concentration; it needs no help.

Give your attention to the still activity of silence.

Brilliance in concentration is the result of interest. When your interest is one hundred per cent, the whole of you is in what you are doing. This is important.

Concentration is fixity of vision, and it is dependent on freedom of action. Let the vagrant thoughts come and go. They are surface reactions, like the waves of the sea. Bless them, but do not resist them. Rather focalize your attention on the depths below, where life is strong, serene and powerful. Progress in concentration is determined more by what you omit than what you retain. It is the process of elimination and drawing together.

PERSISTENCY WILL BE REWARDED

The best progress in this work will be attained by centering your attention upon some attribute of God, or some statement which exemplifies His Nature. Peace is one, and Love is another; tranquility, life, strength, power, joy, health, and happiness. Any of these are good, and it will help you, too, before attempting this work to thoughtfully read over the 189th Psalm or the 13th chapter of I Corinthians. At first, take just one word at a time. Associate yourself with its nature until you receive that which you are declaring. This may take several weeks or even months. No matter; persist until it is yours. Train the mind until it comes to dwell in your consciousness. The mastery of a single word in this manner will greatly strengthen your power of visualization and realization. Then when you have mastered the single word, you can proceed with affirmations of Truth, letting each one take possession of your mind and body. Here are a few to help you:

"I AM Spirit; I think, see, feel, and live as Spirit in the Presence of God, and through the Power of God in me I am able to manifest the Perfection of Spirit in mind and body."

"This Book of the Law shall not depart out of thy mouth, but thou shalt meditate therein day and night, that thou mayest observe to do according to all that is written therein for then thou shalt make thy way prosperous and thou shalt have good success."

"Meditate upon these things, give thyself wholly to them, that thy profiting may appear to all."

"Arise, shine, for thy Light is come and the glory of the Lord is risen upon thee."

"Blessed are they which do hunger and thirst after righteousness, for they shall be filled."

Perfect stillness now pervades my mind and body I am open inwardly to the One Presence and Life of Spirit. This Presence illumines my soul, and fills my Life with all Good, Life, Health, Peace and Prosperity.

"In quietness and confidence shall be my strength."

In this Silence I now surrender all personal limitation, erroneous beliefs and fear. I am One with Universal Good, Harmony and Abundance.

I AM now conscious of the invisible Reality of God and I AM lost in Him.

"God is now revealing Himself unto me by His Spirit—that I may know the things that are freely given to me of God."

In the Silence, I shall take no thought of my needs, for God is my unlimited Supply.

"I AM thy servant; give me understanding that I may know thy testimonies."

"For we know in part and we prophesy in part. But when that which is Perfect is come, then that which is in part shall be done away."

"THE WORD WAS MADE FLESH"

Spirit-filled words are magic, vibrant, living things, but, like food, they must be eaten before they can nourish and sustain. When infused with Spirit they are sacramental in nature and have power. "My words are life to them that find (eat) them, and health to all their flesh." "For it is neither herb nor mollifying plaster that restoreth them to health, but Thy Word, O Lord, which healeth all things." The Word is made flesh and dwells in us whenever we open ourselves to it. Although words be all about us and are not consumed, they do us no good. To open ourselves to Divine words is like opening the gates of an irrigation system, allowing the life-giving water to revive and nourish the parched vegetation that otherwise would perish.

Dietetically speaking, your state of physical health is dependent upon the kind and quality of food you eat. If it is natural it is an ally. If it is unnatural it is an enemy. But how do you appropriate your material food? By the mouth. First you chew it until it has been thoroughly mixed with saliva. Then you swallow it. Entering the stomach, it is again mixed with the gastric juices and finally enters into the substance of the body.

"Man shall not live by bread alone," said Jesus to the tempter, "but by every word that proceedeth out of the mouth of

God." This food is for the Inner or Spiritual man. He, too, has a body and must be fed, but subsisting on only one spiritual meal a week this man is often undernourished and impoverished. If subject to sickness and disease he would have been dead long ago.

Eating is a process of appropriation and digestion, and in the case of the Spiritual man it is a process of appropriating and digesting words. This is His food and must be masticated by attention, fletcherized by meditation, and swallowed by realization. The stomach of the spiritual man is the soul, which is known to psychologists as the receptive or feminine factor, which ingests and digests whatever we give to it. This stomach differs from that in the organic body in that the latter will reject poison or unsuitable food, but the stomach of the Spiritual man digests everything regardless of its nature. It is absolute, and whatever food we eat in this manner becomes our life, producing good or ill.

ABSORB MORE AND AFFIRM LESS

One of the great sins of the human family and one which causes many of our ills is the sin of overeating. This applies to the Spiritual man as well. Most Truth students read too much, affirm too much, and absorb too little. It is far better to take one morsel at a time and digest it thoroughly, than to take a whole book and gulp it. Be selective in your choice of spiritual food. Choose a diet that proceeds from God. Then, "I shall put my Spirit in you, and ye shall live." Take one affirmation at a time and eat of it until it takes root in your soul (subjective mind).

An ancient philosopher said: "Ask not from the Silence, for it cannot speak." This is good advice for all, for many have made and are making the mistake of talking to the Silence. This is as ineffective as to go into a cathedral to carry on a conversation with the building. You go into a church to worship, into a laboratory to experiment, and into the Silence to work. And by work I mean to realize or manifest your Good.

The silent state as I have experienced it is the Residence of God, the place of the Immaculate Conception. It is the focal point where His Spirit bears witness with our spirit and all things become new. You are a majority In the Silence, for you are one with God and whatever you do in this place is done well. If you are seeking a demonstration for another, you mentally take that person with you into the Silence, visualizing him as sitting before you and subject to the same laws. You affirm the Truth for him just as you would for yourself, and by the law of vibration he is affected immediately by every word which you bespeak in his behalf. First call him by name to arouse his subjective mind, and then talk to him as if he were visibly present in the room.

MECHANICS OF THE SILENCE

There is only one satisfactory posture for the Silence, and that is the sitting posture. Choose a stool or bench of sufficient height to allow the feet to rest flat upon the floor. Sit comfortably with head, neck and chest in a perfectly vertical line, and the hands resting loosely upon the thighs with the palms up Make certain the trunk of the body is resting upon the ribs and not on the spinal column.

Select a room if possible that is quiet, one that is remote from noise and strife, and use the same room every day. It is your sanctuary and must be kept untrammeled by the world. Place a table in some conspicuous place and change the cover to correspond in color to the state of mind you wish to induce. Pink vibrates love, violet vibrates Spirit, yellow vibrates wisdom, orange vibrates power, red vibrates life, blue vibrates health and intelligence, green vibrates prosperity and abundance, and blue and orange together vibrate harmony and peace.

Having seated yourself in the position described, you must now tell your body to relax. Start with the top of your head and suggest relaxation to every member of your body. For example, address your face by saying: Every nerve and muscle in my face is relaxed, relaxed, relaxed. Be firm in these suggestions and make each one in a semi-audible voice. Then take the neck, shoulders arms, hands, lungs, liver, stomach, solar plexus, kidneys, spleen, appendix, generative organs, hips, groins, legs, ankles, insteps and toes. Then with each suggestion place your consciousness in the particular member you are relaxing. Flood each one with a deep sense of stillness, and then by the time you reach the toes you will be in a state of perfect physical abstraction. These exercises are important until you have become master of your body, because you cannot receive until you are receptive. This relaxing process is the surrender of body to spirit.

The next step is mastery through breath. The purpose of the breathing exercises is two-fold: First, to establish peace and calm in the nerve centers, bringing them into rhythm with the universal force of Spirit; and second, to eliminate body poisons through oxidation. One exhalation often contains poison to vitiate a barrel of air. When scientifically and faithfully performed, these exercises will remove depression and lassitude from the mind and body, even wrinkles from the face. There is a divine substance in breath which is akin to food, and taking your exercises before breakfast will ofttimes serve as a full meal. Your appetite will have so diminished that you will not desire food.

You can live for days without food, but you can live but briefly without breathing. It is the life of God, and the very substance through which He hears and answers prayer. It was not until God breathed into Adam the Breath of Life that he became a living soul, conscious of spiritual life and being.

Then again in the Bible we have unmistakable evidences and records of the bestowal of gifts and blessings through the process of breathing on people. One of these is recorded in the life of Paul. Coveting for this particular group of people the Truth of the Spirit of God he breathed on them and said: Receive ye the Holy Ghost."

THE LIFE WHICH PENETRATES ALL

This spiritual breath which I am recommending for your use is not the atmospheric breath, but that rarefied substance known as ether. This is the omnipresent breath of God and the life which penetrates all matter. Few know very much about this etheric breath, and most of what is known comes from the far east. But neither do we know much of electricity, though this does not prevent us from using and applying it to our lives. We do know that ether penetrates all substance, including our bodies, and that by an act of faith it can be transmuted into energy, life and health. Think of it as the "water of life," cleansing both your soul and body and washing you clean.

Open your breathing exercises with any one of the following affirmations held steadfastly and feelingly in your mind:

"Not that I am sufficient of myself to think anything as of myself; but my sufficiency is of God."

The Breath of God is my Life.

The Breath of God is omnipresent. It now washes my body clean.

I now inhale this Breath and I am quickened, renewed, vitalized and strengthened.

In this Spiritual Breath of God which now surges through my being, I am young, whole and free.

> Breathe on me, Breath of God;
>   Fill me with Life anew,
> That I may love what Thou dost love,
>   And do what Thou wouldst do.
>
> Breathe on me, Breath of God,
>   Until my heart is pure;
> Until with Thee I will one will,
>   To do or to endure.
>
> Breathe on me, Breath of God,
>   Till I am wholly Thine;
> Till all this earthly part of me
>   Glows with Thy fire divine.
>
> Breathe on me, Breath of God,
>   So shall I never die;
> But live with Thee the Perfect Life
>   Of Thine eternity.

—No. 380, Episcopal Hymnal.

The Infinite Life of Spirit is now surging through my body, cleansing me of all impurity.

There is but one mind, the Mind of Christ. There is but one body, the Body of God. There is but one energy, the Energy of Spirit, and I am one with all there is.

I AM: one with the Trinity of God. I AM indivisible, unhurtable, fearless and immune. There is nothing to deny or treat, for I AM that I AM, an embodiment of the One Life and Being.

God is God, Christ is Christ, Spirit is Spirit, and Life is Life. I AM Life, because I AM that which is, Perfect individual and glorious being.

In the Power of the Holy Ghost I AM now liberated from all false beliefs and delusions. I ascend in my Spiritual body, filled with joy and Light.

When you are certain that you are abstract, relaxed and still, then flex every muscle in your body as tightly as you can. Squeeze every atom of your being just as you would squeeze a dry sponge in a bucket of water to make it absorbent. Then relax and repeat the exercise twice more. Now breathe deeply five or six times in rapid succession and come to a complete pause. When you feel rested then you are ready to breathe in rhythm. This is done by making your inhalations deep, slow and quiet, and then by throwing into vibration on each exhalation any one of the foregoing affirmations.

Or take some word which comprehends Deity. Metaphysicians and many others like the word om, the first two letters of the three words, omnipresent, omnipotent and omniscient, from the Latin word omni, meaning all. Using this, the exercise would be something like this: Inhale while mentally counting 1, 2, 3, 4, 5, 6, 7; exhale and throw into vibration the word om — o-m-m-m-m-m-m. Repeat this breath three times and during each repetition feel the Life of the Spirit permeating every part of your body. If at first the counts are too long, cut them down. This exercise may be used with any one of the declarations in this book, though you will have to extend the counts on the exhalation. Give absolute attention to every word and open every avenue of expression. Thinking with God in the One Mind of Christ will bring upon you the baptism of the Holy Spirit, commonly called the Epiphany (showing forth) of the perfection of your body and mind.

If you are a novice in this work your mind will wander in many directions at once. Do not be disturbed by the detours and do not resist them. Simply do as you would if your automobile was headed for some distant city and persisted in getting off the main road. Keep bringing it back until it is established in the pulsing Life of Spirit.

AVOID TENSION OF MIND OR BODY

Watch your mind and body for tenseness. Spirit never struggles and is never tense. The more abstract and relaxed you become, without tension in either mind or body, the more power and illumination you will draw into your life. The success of all demonstrations in the Silence is dependent upon a profound mental and physical passivity and receptivity, though never at any time will your mind be blank, for it is impossible to think of nothing. "'Tis the set of the sail, and not the gale, that bids us where to go."

The next step is to open the silence. This is always done with the cosmic, universal Lord's Prayer: "Our Father which art in Heaven, Hallowed be Thy Name. Thy Kingdom come, Thy will be done in earth, as it is in Heaven. Give us this day our daily bread. And forgive us our trespasses, as we forgive those who trespass against us. And lead us not into temptation, but deliver us from evil; for Thine is the kingdom, and the power, and the glory, forever. Amen."

Now get your spiritual focus through communion with Spirit. Affirm your desire for cosmic consciousness (the Kingdom of Heaven). Keep your vision one-pointed and you will perceive that vision coming toward you. Finally you will merge into it and become a part of it. Repeat inaudibly with great conviction, "Behold I (the Christ consciousness) make all things new!"

Take courage from the experience of St. Augustine, who, after he had apparently met every condition, related his experience in the following words: "My mind withdrew its thought from experience, exacting itself from the contradictory throng of sensuous images, that it might find out what that light was wherein it was bathed; and then with a flash of one hurried glance, it attained to the vision of that which is. Then at last I saw Thy invisible things that are made, but I could not sustain my gaze; my weakness was dashed back (conscious interruption), and I was relegated to my ordinary experience, bearing with me only a loving memory and, as it were, the fragrance of these desirable meats on the which as yet I was not able to feed."

NONE CAN KEEP IT FROM YOU BUT YOURSELF

Mastery of the Silence is not easy, for it is a climb to God. You may stumble many times and have many failures, but the summit is the reward of persistence. It is won only by the dauntless. Even after many months you may get only glimpses. Do not be dismayed and do not give up. It is participation you are seeking, not observation. The Truth is for you, and no one can keep it from you but yourself. The more you practice, the more supple your consciousness becomes. Gradually you will unfold into that high realm of knowledge and wisdom which passeth understanding. Like Jesus, you will know with no conscious study, and heal with no conscious effort. "You shall mount up with wings as eagles," you "shall run and not be weary," you "shall walk and not faint."

Says Christian D. Larson in Science of Mind: "Every step that is taken in the raising of consciousness means more life, greater intelligence, greater freedom, greater demonstration, greater realization, more brilliant thinking and higher knowing. And when we go far enough in the raising of consciousness, we shall enter the home of the soul; we shall enter the unending Silence of the Spirit; we shall enter the peace that passeth understanding; we shall enter cosmic consciousness; we shall enter the realm of spiritual reality, where all things are perfect; we shall enter the cosmos of the limitless, where all power is given; we shall enter life itself — the Life Everlasting — where immortality is discovered; we shall enter the light of Divine Intelligence — the Brilliance of pure wisdom — where all things are known.

"Thus we understand the full and high meaning of this remarkable statement: 'Be still — and know.' The farther we go into spiritual stillness, the more we shall know; and when we go far enough, we shall enter that light wherein anything may be known—even to know that 'I AM God;' and this can only mean that we may in that Secret Place, meet the Most High face to face; that we may actually look in upon that marvelous realm 'where the Infinite abides in smiling repose.' " This realm, designated as "The Fourth Dimension," I shall touch upon in another book.

THINGS TO REMEMBER ABOUT THE SILENCE

The most wonderful Spiritual work is done in the great eternal calm.

Silence does not mean inactivity, but a perfect activity.

The Silence is a process of entering into Oneness with Universal Law.

The more profound your Silence, the more effective it becomes.

The movement of the Silence is imperceptible; the higher the force the more still it becomes.

The Silence is power, the power to demonstrate the Truth.

The mind in the Silence creates that on which it concentrates.

The nature of the Silence is order. It is the mill of Spirit, objectifying that which is conceived.

The Silence makes real your possibilities only when you claim them.

In the Silence, you are thinking in Universal Mind.

Stilling the sense of life is turning on the Light.

When you are absolutely still you are empty, and good flows into you.

The Silence contains all that you desire.

To treat another in the Silence is to bring him into union with God.

Sleep in the Silence implies indolence and negation. If you are troubled with insomnia, take your Silence at night with the special intention of sleep.

The supreme and indispensable requirements for a perfect Silence are Universal Love, Trust, and absolute stillness within and without.

Always bless others while you are in the Silence, sending out healing or prosperity thoughts to the whole world.

Keep your interest at flood tide until your Silence is ended.

Do not make the mistake of practicing too long. Once the contact has been made, you will know intuitively when you have finished.

HEALING IN THE SILENCE

To save divinely is to love divinely. Thus the supreme attitude in all healing is Love. God is Love. It is the subtle touch of spirit, and as you silently send it forth you are reaching out with your thousands of tiny nerve hands to quicken with cleansing and recovery the object of your choice. True Love is strong enough to meet any condition. It is immutable and unchangeable, the final essence in all salvation.

Having found the affirmative factor in healing, we shall now inquire as to its nature and the conditions for healing. First, there must be a great desire in the patient to be healed. He must want it as badly as a drowning man wants air. Sincere desire is like the "leaven which a woman took and hid in three measures of meal until the whole was leavened." Faith takes hold of the Love which you release and transmutes it into life.

Love always judges righteously. It looks above that which is diseased and corrupt and sees only that which is Perfect. As long as the healer is cognizant of destruction and imperfection he cannot do the patient any good. New-found strength and health is not perceived in the image of weakness, but in the image of strength. Jesus in healing beheld nothing but perfection. If a man came to Him with a withered hand, He saw not the infirmity, but visualized only that which God had created, and which was perfect.

Whether the patient be with you or a thousand miles away, Christian healing is perfected by the law of vibration. Therefore the best results are always obtained when the patient is en rapport with Spirit and healer. The subjective mind of the patient cannot receive what you have to give him until he is attuned. There must be two souls in the same pitch.

45

"If there are two pianos in the room, keyed to the same pitch, the vibrations of the one struck produce in the other echoes of the same tones."

Everything in the universe is in a constant state of vibration — electricity, heat, sound, light, color, motion, music, odor — all are made real by vibration. But the highest vibration and that which travels at the greatest speed is the vibration of spiritualized thought. Piercing in its power, it annihilates distance and touches the very heart of God.

Thus, if your patient is unified, every word you speak in his behalf touches him with lightning speed, instantly. Working through the two great centers of the universe he becomes the inlet and outlet for all there is in God.

In the full confidence of Spirit you will first call your patient by name to arrest his attention and to open his subjective mind. Do this three times:

"Mary! Mary! Mary!"

Claim her full attention by telling her that you love her and that God loves her. Tell her that you have come to claim His Good for her and that she must listen to every word. Then when you feel intuitively that you have the listening attitude, affirm to yourself: The All-Knowing Mind of God works through my mind and in His Love this child (Mary) is made whole. Realize your oneness with Life and that you are a conscious distributing center of this life. Send it forth as a great sweeping cleansing tide to your patient, saying:

"Mary, I offer you strength, life and abundance. It is the gift of God, your gift, and you must claim it now."

By this time you have opened the fountains of healing and you must wait in the stillness for the manifestation of spirit. From now on you should speak only those words which He presses into your consciousness. These will be the words of life and, since you are but the instrument, you must let Him speak through you. At first you may need affirmations of your own. Use them; but eventually you must come to that place in consciousness where you are willing to let Spirit do the speaking.

When the treatment is ended, sit for five or ten minutes in absolute realization of the fulfillment of what you have asked. Conclude the treatment by thanking God for the answer for that which has been done in His Name. I like to use the words either before or after the treatment: "In the Name of the Father, and of the Son, and of the Holy Ghost. Amen. So let it be." Amen was the god of generation.

HEALING STATEMENTS

God in me is robust health, strength and power. Holiness is healthiness, therefore I AM healthy, even as God is healthy.

The healing Mind of Christ now fills me with the Presence of Truth, and I am free from bondage.

The Omnipresent Life of Spirit now permeates my body and I AM every whit whole.

The newness of the Christ Life now surges through my body, harmonizing, vitalizing and recreating every atom of my being.

I AM a living prism, revealing the Light of God in perfection and beauty.

The I AM of Spirit now clarifies my vision, and I perceive only that which is perfect.

"Abiding in the Christ Mind, His Word is made flesh in my body."

The Great eternal Light of Spirit now illumines my body and I AM cleansed of all error.

The Wholeness of Spirit now quickens my mortal body.

The Word of God in me is triumphant, abounding health and peace.

The freedom of the Christ Mind now liberates me from all sickness and in harmony.

My consciousness is now filled with the healing power of Christ. In His Name I AM unified with Truth.

Through the Salvation of God in Christ, I am saved from disease.

My body now bears witness to the Truth that God is All.

Looking away from that which is corrupt, I behold only that which is perfect.

Laying off the soiled garments of death, I now

clothe myself in the wedding garments of health.

My heritage is health, and the tendency of my body is perfection. I claim these now in consciousness.

The Order and Harmony of the Christ Life is now established in my body, strengthening every cell and fibre, and expressing Itself as perfect health.

PROSPERITY STATEMENTS

Divine Goodness now manifests in me as my unfailing supply.

The prosperity which I desire to express is now present in me.

The riches of the Christ Mind now manifest in my mind, and I accept that which is for my highest good.

The abundance of the Infinite Mind is now established in my consciousness, and I do not lack.

I rejoice in the abundance of God which is now made manifest in my affairs.

I am a vacuum of unlimited supply, and the abundance of God pours in on me.

The increase of Spirit now multiplies my loaves and fishes, and I am prosperous.

Divine supply is my unfailing source of good.

"My God shall supply all your need according to His riches in Glory by Christ Jesus."

The all-sufficient Christ Mind now fills my cup to overflowing with prosperity.

Since there is no separation in Spirit, I am one with unlimited supply. My good flows to me from every direction.

GOD THE FATHER

Metaphysical speculators have defined God as Principle. This definition is good as far as it goes, but we cannot stop at Principle. Jesus who came to reveal the Nature of God, taught us to say: "Our Father," and Moses in the first chapter of Genesis said: "Man is made in the image and likeness of God."

Principle means beginning or cause. It is unchangeable and eternal. True, God is Harmony, Unity, Love, Activity and Perfection, but He is more than the sum total of all His Principles. He is "Our Father," three Persons, One God, Alpha and Omega, without beginning and without end.

It is God the Father, or no God at all. And my claim for the personality of the Godhead is not based upon the age-old concept of an anthropomorphic individual of huge proportions. Personality does not consist of complexion, form, hands, feet, head, eyes or expression, but of consciousness, in other words, anyone who can say "I AM." Joseph Cook says: "There cannot be thought without a thinker; there is thought in the universe; there is therefore a Thinker in the universe.

But a thinker is a person, therefore there is a personal Thinker in the universe." The same thought was expressed by Locke, who said: "We must consider what personal stands for, which I think is a thinking, intelligent being, that has reason and reflection, and that can consider itself as itself — the same thinking in different times and places." Give me a God who is conscious of my needs, One who knows and loves and One who is available for my every need.

Principle of itself is cold, sterile and impersonal, void of interest or care. Away with such a doctrine! Give me the God of Christ, One who can guide, think, feel and redeem; One to whom I can talk when I am in trouble, sickness or sin. Let us consider the psychology of God as Person and worship Him as our Father.

JESUS CHRIST

"The man Jesus Christ is the Word of God Incarnate."

Jesus claimed to be the virgin-born Son of God — "the Way, the Truth and the Life" — and proved this claim by His works. To say that He never claimed to be God is blasphemy, and violates the statement of Isaiah who said that when the virgin-born Messiah came, He was to be called God with us, and the statement of Jesus in the Garden of Gethsemane who called Himself by the name Adoni, the I AM. Immediately the soldiers fell on their faces in wonder and awe. Jesus was the only man in history who ever dared to use this sacred Name of God, first spoken to Moses from the flaming bush. To deny the divinity of Jesus Christ is to deny God. This claim you remember was the compelling argument for His death. For this alone — that He called Himself God — was He crucified.

Jesus Christ is the I AM in the flesh, and His ministry is summed up in the words: "I am come to seek and to save that which was lost." Calvary is the great fulcrum by which the world is lifted.

SICKNESS

To get away from sickness you must get out of mortal, or flesh mind. This mind (objective) was by Christ referred to as "the world." "In the world ye shall have tribulation; but be of good cheer, I have overcome the world."

Sickness is "false belief," but true or false, it is real. And since belief presupposes mind, there must be a consciousness which corresponds to any condition in the body. Since it has no quality apart from mind, it cannot get sick by itself. Did you ever hear of a corpse contracting pneumonia, small-pox or diphtheria? Contagion has no effect whatsoever upon a mindless body, therefore it is the consciousness of disease which makes it real.

The Bible does not say that a man shall not get sick, but it does show him the way to get well. If there was nothing to get sick, then there would be nothing to treat and no need for a practitioner. Sickness is real only to sense, and the mind which records sense. It is not sent upon us, but comes in a permissive sense, just as sin comes to us. And to deny it is to recognize it.

Now since disease and pain depend for their existence upon mind, they are real. Rheumatism is rheumatism, goitre is goitre, and tumor is tumor. Everything is just as real as it is supposed to be, and you cannot destroy it by pretty terms.

There is only one thing that will remove sickness, and that is change—a change of consciousness. The chemistry which makes us sick and the chemistry which makes us well is all centered in the mind. It is the reciprocal action between mind and body that is called correspondence. The latter is the mirror of the former.

Contrary to the teachings and beliefs of many, there is a law of disease just as there is a law of ease, and both are laws unto themselves. To tell the deaf man that he is not deaf is malpractice, and serves to fasten his deafness upon him.

The true way to heal sickness is to separate yourself from the mind of the flesh, or as Jesus said, "to come out of the world." As a child of God the tendency of your body is toward perfection, but perfection is manifested only in the Christ Mind. This Mind will not only change your body, but your habits also.

"I AM the resurrection and the life," saith the Lord; "whosoever liveth and believeth in Me, though he were dead, yet shall he live; and whosoever liveth and believeth in Me shall never die."

"Thou art my glorious health, and in Thee I express physical and mental perfection."

THE CONSCIOUS MIND

In reality man has only one mind, but since it manifests on three different planes it is classified as conscious, subconscious and superconscious. Other classifications of the mind are objective, subjective and spirit mind, world consciousness, self consciousness and God consciousness. The three co-exist, one with the other.

The conscious mind is the surface mind — that part of your mentality which knows itself. As indicated elsewhere in this book, it is the mind of sense, or the region of tangibility. Being in the world it is that part of mind which is farthest away from God, recording only that which He has done in the deeper regions of another plane. Being the mind of the flesh, God is never present in your conscious mind. "Flesh and blood cannot inherit the Kingdom of Heaven."

Conscious activity is the seat of imagination, reason, will, sense, judgments, ideas, convictions, conclusions, and, in fact, all voluntary action. Reasoning deductively, its mentation is always weak. Acting on the surface, it is subject to illusion, and is unstable and unreliable. This is the department of mind which needs control. If too active at night it will prevent sleep. Much of our present day insomnia and neurasthenia is due to too much conscious activity at night when the physical man is still. The only way to slow down conscious activity is through mental relaxation and rest. Allowing the conscious mind to run riot after you retire is carrying tomorrow's load with today's energy.

SUBCONSCIOUS MIND

The great field of mental action designated as "the world within" is the subconscious, unconscious or subliminal mind. It is the great reactionary instrument to consciousness. The conscious mind formulates plans, and the subconscious mind executes them. Or as has been said: "Consciousness is the architect and subconsciousness is the builder."

The subconscious is far more important than the conscious, since it controls every vital function of the body and never sleeps. In common parlance, the subconscious is your best friend. It is the seat of power, intuition, telepathy, kinetic energy, emotions, memory, and all supra-normal cognitions. Abiding in this mind you become automatic or natural. As it is the feminine factor of mind we must be careful what we project into it. Reasoning and functioning inductively, it gives back to us whatever we put into it, for the conscious mind can create disease, and the subconscious mind can establish it or eradicate it. Working through cause and effect, the subconscious mind mirrors in the body whatever is given it.

This subconscious mind, which carries on more than eighty-five per cent of our mental processes, does its best work at night, when all interference from the conscious mind is removed. Thus in natural sleep great things may be evolved. Being your servant, you must command it to work for you while you sleep. Co-existing or working complementary to the conscious and superconscious, it is related to every department of life, and through its power there is nothing that can not be accomplished.

THE SUPERCONSCIOUS MIND

The Superconscious mind is God, that "something in man which was never born, is never sick, and never dies." Call this something what you will, it is none the less Supreme Knowingness of your Godhood, the Holy Spirit, which is your inherent capacity to be and to do. Living in this mind you are called Spiritual, in the subconscious mind you are called natural, and in the conscious mind you are called carnal. As Auberlen says: "Body, soul and spirit are nothing else than the real basis of the three elements of man's being, world consciousness, self consciousness and God consciousness. The Spirit or superconsciousness then, is your ego, the I AM of God which comprehends and manifests His Good.

Unifying your superconsciousness with the Superconsciousness of God is bringing yourself into Oneness with Universal Law. "As many as received Him, to them gave He power to become the sons of God, even to them that believe on His Name; which were born, not of blood, nor of the will of the flesh, nor of the will of man, but of God."

The superconscious mind of man touched by the Spirit (Superconscious Mind) of God, makes you son. It is the rebirth termed by St. Paul as a "renewing of the Spirit of the mind," as a "partaking of the Divine Nature," and by St. Peter as a "spiritual resurrection." "Strengthened with might by His Spirit in the inner man" means that every increase, every renewal, and every regeneration in man comes through the Superconscious activity of God. Thus Superconscious Life is the full life. To be God-conscious is to be God-filled.

CONSCIOUSNESS

Consciousness is awareness. It is a movement of mind in mind which knows itself as of itself. It is the great perceiver relating man to his environment. To become conscious of anything you become aware of it, one with it. But there is an inner and outer awareness. The first relates you to Spirit (Superconsciousness) and the second relates you to flesh. As you have already seen, these states are designated as Cosmic (Christ) Consciousness and ordinary or world consciousness.

To become conscious of anything is to know that thing and to be able to understand it, to become one with it. But consciousness, like muscle, grows with use. You become great according to your unfoldment of consciousness. Your consciousness of water is very limited in infancy; it is only something wet, something to drink. You are only partially conscious of its significance. Then as you grow older you become aware of its larger usefulness, and the many ways in which it is used by man. In reality water is like the air, which has to be mastered, but this mastery depends upon an ever-expanding consciousness.

So with all else in life; the only things we can master are those which we have in consciousness. This is the best explanation of evolution, for the progress of mankind is but the story of an evoluted consciousness.

GIVING AND RECEIVING

There is a law of giving as there is a law of receiving. "Give and it shall be given unto you; good measure, pressed down, shaken together, running over, shall men give into your bosom. For with what measure ye mete it shall be measured to you again."

The person who is avaricious, acquisitive, stingy, is in a world by himself, isolated, separated. He cannot receive Spiritual gifts. "God loveth a cheerful giver," as illustrated in the story of the widow's mite. In the eyes of Jesus, her gift was greatest because she had given her best, her all.

The desire to hoard and to possess is a besetting sin, always fraught with dire consequences. Charles Fillmore says:

"Avarice grips the arms and legs, shriveling them with paralysis. It sends its tremendous currents of fear of loss or lack to the stomach, and men starve with plenty at hand. With its hot desire to possess, it fills the body with fever, and when failure and loss come uppermost, the reaction causes a wide whirl of insanity to surge through the brain." The person who hoards or withholds is damming his good. If prompted by fear and uncertainty of the future it is lack — lack of faith. Indeed it is faith in evil which is so aptly illustrated by the miser. Even though he have millions he is still poor.

Mental receptivity is determined by generosity, and since money is the same substance as that which heals, there is virtue in giving. Every time we give we are being healed. Therefore we should give as we expect to receive, for until the consciousness has been opened there can be no quickening. "It is more blessed to give than to receive," said the Master Giver. Hence nothing expands the soul like the exercise of giving. Put yourself into your gift and you will reap bountifully. It was said of Cleveland Dodge, one of America's greatest philanthropists, "that wherever his money went, Mr. Dodge was sure to go."

THE KINGDOM OF HEAVEN

"I go to prepare a place for you .... that where I AM, there ye may be also." In the past we have visualized this place as a city in the skies, something to be reached by death. We have sung about it as the "Beautiful Isle of Somewhere" and thought of it as "over there," remote and distant from present life. In reality it is not "over" at all, but "under." I refer to that sub-stratum of consciousness already defined as subjectivity. We are already immortal, for the spiritual body exists now. What we think of as in the "sweet by and by" is the continuity of consciousness and the persistence of our objective faculties.

"Lo! I AM With you always," said Jesus. Now, if the I AM of understanding is with us always, how can He be absent from us? The mansions that have been prepared for us are the many states of consciousness, where Christ dwells. Thus when we raise the mental level to these mansions we come into possession of them. We are dwellers in Truth.

The incarnate Form of Jesus Christ on earth was just as much in Heaven as He is now. Being in tune with, or related to First Cause He was in God, and God was in Him. And my authority for this statement is Jesus.

All things are ready — now! And you will never be one bit closer to Heaven than you are at the present moment. This was the great burden of the Sacred Heart, to bring His children into the quickening realization of the Kingdom now! The Promised Land is within you, but like Love or Peace, you can not see it save with spiritual eyes. "The Kingdom of God cometh not by observation." On the contrary, the Kingdom consciousness is registered in mind, where it manifests its power and dominion.

If you are waiting and watching for the Kingdom of Heaven in death, you are delaying your good, for when death of the body comes you will have to start all over. The only treasures you will have on the next plane are those which you take in consciousness from this plane. Until God dwells in your consciousness here you will never be in Heaven.

HUMAN POISONS

"A man's enemies," says the prophet, "are the men of his own house." These enemies are legion, and always emanate from discordant states of mind. Harmful as tobacco, narcotics and alcohol are to the human body, they are negligible as compared to the mental wreckers of worry, fretting, malice, fear, grief, criticism, unbridled passions, jealousy, envy, lust, and discontent. "There is not a thought that is not striking a blow; there is not an impulse that is not doing mason work; there is not a passion that is not a workman's thrust. There are as many master workmen in you as there are separate faculties, and there are as many blows being struck as there are separate acts of emotion."

Let us turn the searchlight of truth upon some of these blighting thoughts. The first I would mention is fear. "Fear hath torment," says the Bible. It is the incubator of every disease, and the most prolific source of mental and physical derangement. No part of the human body is immune to its ravages. It weakens, blights, curses, destroys and poisons the whole system. The fearful man is always a sick man, and what he really fears seldom overtakes him. "Fear not " is the high command of Jesus.

Next to fear comes worry. Oh, that I had words to tell you about this worst of all mental diseases! Without doubt it is the most fatal and damnable of all our errors. Wasting as it does the very energy of life, it vitiates every gland, tissue and action of the body. It dims the eye, and slows down the heart. It is like a swinging door, constantly in motion but never getting anywhere. If you are beset with worry, for your own sake read the sixth chapter of Matthew and the thirty-seventh Psalm. Since your Heavenly Father is your supply, and "knoweth that ye have need of these things," why should you worry? Cast your burden upon the Lord and let go of it.

Know this: When you fall below par mentally, disintegration sets in and physical depression follows. Be jealous, critical, malicious and hateful if you choose, but remember that "whatsoever a man soweth that shall he also reap." If you sow in discord you will reap destruction. The penalty is sure and swift, and no one can escape it.

HUMAN TONICS

The great antidotes for mental and physical poisons are the things of the Spirit. God is Love. It is the surplus of spirit; and what poison tears down, love will build up. Where love is there is no lack. Residing in the subconscious mind, its stimulating, quickening and equalizing force is distributed to every cell and fibre of the body.

Another tonic is Faith. "Faith is the substance of things hoped for, the evidence of things not seen." Whatever you have faith in you endow with power. Concrete faith is dynamic and fulfilling. It translates God into form. "According to your faith, be it done unto you." Faith in God releases God.

Happiness, too, is medicine. Try it for your depression. Health is harmony, and dis-ease is discord. Thus a body full of harmony can not be sick. Fill every organ with happiness and you will generate virility, and disease which has already. possessed you will depart.

Get the Smile habit! Relax your body in smiles. It is much easier than frowning. It only takes thirteen muscles of the face to make a smile and sixty-five to make a frown. Nothing so stimulates the cells of the body, the nerves, digestion and elimination as mental and physical happiness. Give happiness suggestions to your subconscious mind. Awaken and circulate better thoughts. Be firm, resolute and optimistic, and you will have greater efficiency.

Eliminate stimulants in food and drink. Supplant them with rejuvenated foods. Raise your physical octaves by psycho-physical breathing, sun baths, water and exercise. After all, life will be just as colorful as you make it.

Other health-bringers are gratitude, kindness and hope, three of the great sacraments of life. The kindly person is like a "tree planted by the rivers of water, that bringeth forth his fruit in his season; his leaf also shall not wither; and whatsoever he doeth shall prosper." Kindness is a balm that soothes the whole man.

Hope is to man what the accelerator is to the automobile. And when this hope is centered in God, man is supported by the future. Hope accelerates the heart action, relieves nervous tension and gives new strength.

Also, we must be grateful, for gratitude is one of the great magnetic poles of attraction. When you are deeply thankful, you are physically open and receptive. The practice daily of sincere expressions of gratitude for what you already have brings more. Therefore start each day with a thankful heart. Open your body and let the sunshine in. Greet each morning with a song, like the birds, and you will be happy all day long.

PROCRASTINATION

Do not put off until this afternoon what you can do this morning. Procrastination in the performance of any task is waste. It is dissipation of the energy which is needed for your advancement. Professor James spoke of it as "the agony of beginning a task."

The easy road is the popular one to the majority of mortals. What can be done tomorrow need not be done today, we say. It is our nature to follow the line of least resistance. Thus we go to warm climates in the winter and cool climates in the summer. We dread the effort of meeting resistance, the dread of beginning what needs to be done, and the lost motion is always waste. It leads eventually to inertia, which is always a state of death. And, of course, procrastination implies a lack of interest. No matter how busy we may be, how many things we have to do, there is always time to do that we really want to do. We will slip it in somewhere.

From a health standpoint, you will find that the hard road in the beginning is always the easy road in the end. Fight postponement and delay as you would a fire in your house. Make use of the momentum which you lose in getting ready to do the task and the task will literally do or perform itself.

Procrastinators accomplish very little. They spend most of their energy in low or second gear, and wear themselves out by too many stops and starts. If the engine of your automobile is cold it takes twice, possibly three times, as much gasoline and battery power to start it as when it is warm. The human mental engine is equally refractory. If you have something to do or some task to perform, do not waste your energy by dreading or postponing it. Rather conserve that strength by immediate action. Tasks cease to be tasks only when you get at them, and fill them with enthusiasm. Check up each day and determine if you have disposed of everything that could be disposed of in that day. Don't carry them from one day to another.

CRITICISM

Adders, crocodiles, scorpions, basilisks, ticks, mosquitoes, yellow fever and typhoid — put them all together and you have a miscellaneous melange of menaces to human health and security. What an effect they have upon humanity, yet how mild in comparison to that more insidious monster, criticism. Though the Bible warns we shall be held accountable "for every idle word," freely we indulge in the pernicious practice of spreading disease through misrepresentation, slander, back-biting and fault-finding. The chronic critic is a menace to himself, to his church, his community, his lodge, his friends, his business, to everybody who comes into the range of his influence. He whispers, damns, debauches and poisons; no person or thing is immune from his attack. He is the author of trouble, the spreader of discontent, the destroyer of life. His tongue is a lash — hard, cruel and relentless.

Criticism is a defense weapon, but always retroactive. Like the boomerang in the hands of the Australian primitive, it returns to the wielder, often more potent to cause injury to himself than to his intended victim. It is an admission of lost control, a mind out of gear, a life running wild. Psychoanalysts are terming it a form of possession. When you feel impelled to belittle another, pause; remember that other is but a mirror reflecting you; that you see in him what you have within yourself. If there were not a capacity in yourself which corresponds to the evil in others you could not behold it.

"Either how canst thou say to thy brother, Brother, let me pull out the mote that is in thine eye, when thou thyself beholdest not the beam that is in thine own eye? Thou hypocrite, cast out first the beam out of thine own eye, and then shalt thou see clearly to pull out the mote that is in thy brother's eye."

"A good man, out of the good treasure of his heart, bringeth forth that which is good; and an evil man out of the evil treasure of his heart bringeth forth that which is evil: for of the abundance of the heart his mouth speaketh. " Cosmic vision beholds always the positive, that which is good, and has approval for everything. This is well illustrated by an incident in the life of Jesus. With His disciples He came one day upon the dead body of a dog. Decomposition had set in, and disregarding the exclamations of the disciples who apparently could not endure the odor, Jesus paused by the body, and with his staff parting the lips, spoke of the symmetry and beauty of the canine teeth. Even in a decaying carcass He found something beautiful and fine. Think of the lesson here. Approval and appreciation are the solvents of negation and criticism. Scissors alone will never make or mend a garment. It takes needle and thread.

When tempted to criticise anyone or anything, even mildly, if you will pause for a moment to forget the evil and look for the good, there will always be some quality in that person or thing which you can approve. Whatever good you find in others will day by day come to dwell in you.

Someone has said that a dollar saved is a dollar earned. I shall paraphrase that aphorism by saying a criticism crushed is a victory won. Commend everybody and everything—your children, your home, your church, your town, your state, your nation, your food. The good is there, but only you can bring it out. And, since you can hold only one thought at a time, make it a good one. Admire others and they will admire you. There are only two courses in life from which to choose: Christ or chaos. "I, if I be lifted up, will draw all men unto me." The world can never belong to you as long as you are negative. Let there be a lifting up!

FORGIVENESS

"Father, forgive them, for they know not what they do."

Nothing so inhibits spiritual growth and unfoldment as unforgiveness. Grudges overshadow you and hold you in chains, mentally, physically and spiritually. And the only person I pity is the one who is so short-sighted and woefully ignorant as to carry a grudge or bitterness in his consciousness to the next world. What is bound on earth is bound in heaven, and what fetters us here fetters us there.

"Where the tree falleth, there it shall be." Life on the next plane is a continuation of life here. Thus a man who carries through the veil of death bitterness in his soul is only hampering his own progress; he is earthbound. Our prayer, "Forgive us our trespasses," is meaningless until we have fulfilled the conditions of the remainder of the sentence "as we forgive those who trespass against us." Reconciliation is one of the first requisites to answered prayer. How can we expect forgiveness from Christ until we have first forgiven those who have committed offenses toward us? Whomsoever you bar through unforgiveness, shall be a barrier in your path.

As long as Job rebelled and fought, his misery increased; it was only when he prayed for those who had trespassed against him that their power over him ended. If someone has injured you, pour out your love and blessings upon him. Drop the bitterness from your mind and the evil will cease to exist. Forgiveness is your breastplate of protection. And every time you drop a hurt by burning it up in Divine Love, you are rising in consciousness, and the higher you go the smaller the grievances become. It is the difference between looking at men from the level of the street, and viewing them from a skyscraper. Writing the faults of others in the sand is one of the fine arts of living. It must be cultivated assiduously. But let us remember there is no forgiveness without forgetfulness. How many times I have heard: "Well, I can forgive, but I can never forget." Ah, there is the rub! There is no valid forgiveness until the injury is forgotten. If you are still holding in memory that which has hurt you, you have not forgiven.

"If we confess our sins, He is faithful and just to forgive us our sins and to cleanse us from all unrighteousness." Blessed God! In Him every need is met. The promise is forgiveness, absolution and freedom. Hear His words: "Behold, thou art made whole: sin no more, lest a worse thing come unto thee."

The catholic doctrine of absolution is psychologically sound, but a confession can become efficacious only when the penitent one stops his sinning. Forgiveness is consummated only when we are truly converted (turned about). This fact is clearly and dramatically illustrated in the parable of the prodigal son. Study it carefully and you will see that forgiveness is not mentioned. Now when the prodigal son realized his situation he said: "I will arise and go to my father and will say unto him: Father, I have sinned against Heaven and in thy sight, and am no more worthy to be called thy son; make me as one of thy hired servants." Return to the father's house was a sufficient confession of his unworthiness, and the story indicates that the father did not even listen to his self-torture and morbid introspection, for while he was yet speaking the father commanded the servants to bring gifts. Self-condemnation is a characteristic trait of humanity as it passes from sense to soul, but it is always destructive and fixes rather than eliminates error. The significant thing in this great parable is the unmistakable fact that we are forgiven only when we turn ourselves about and stop our sinning. Any sense of incompletion is always in the human and not in the Divine. Redemption and forgiveness are conditional. All that is necessary is to return to the Father. When we turn toward God, God turns toward us. If we act as though He were, we shall know that He is.

THE DIVINE ALCHEMIST

"Therefore if any man be in Christ, he is a new creature old things are passed away; behold, all things are become new!"

Commerce with Christ is the fundamental need of every man. To deny this need is to shut himself away from it. Just as a little flower by the roadside needs the sky, the rain, the wind and the sun, so man needs the infinity of God to fulfill his destiny. It is a large demand to make, but it is a fundamental law of being. You and Christ have business with each other. Shutting yourself away from this Central Intelligence is inhibiting your growth. You may say you want nothing to do with Christ, that you do not need Him in your life. You can, through the accumulation of things, barricade yourself so that He never reaches you, but everything about you will show that you are denying this law of your being. Your face will show it. Your eyes will show it. Your blood and your skin will show that you have shut Christ out of your life.

Christ Consciousness is the Divine Alchemist of your being. But it is one thing to be in Christ and quite another thing to have Christ in you. Often it means very little when a man says he has been through a university, but quite another thing if he says the university has been through him. The highest manifestations of education come through the university that is within.

We live in an orderly universe, and Spirit is power. To become the master you are potentially is to have Christ within, at your center. The without becomes as the within through an invisible law known as transmutation. Christ manifests in you only as you transmute or lift Him up in your consciousness. It is a process which St. Paul spoke of as "dying daily." By the operation of this law you transform the lesser or unregenerate emotions and thoughts of your life into those which are positive and ennobling. Condemnation and commendation are the negative and positive poles of the same power. If by a persistent and sincere conscious effort you seize every impulse to condemn, and by the compelling force of the Christ Within transmute the condemnatory attitude into one of commendation, you will find that you are becoming a new creature in Christ. It is much like an elevator which, through the force of electricity, pulls the weights down and lifts the cage up. The elevator cannot go up until the weights come down. Condemnation, hate, criticism, envy, bitterness, fear and sorrow all comprise the weights — the old man. Pulling these down through the law of transmutation (dying daily) you lift their positive qualities up. Whenever the old man in you begins to assert himself, recognize at once that you are allowing your carnal mind to pervert the power of your spiritual mind. Never allow any hurtful impulse to endure after its inception. It is much easier to control a moth in the egg than when it is flying about. Kill these impulses by the intelligent expression of the desirable impulses. A draft of air in summer refreshes and stimulates you, but the same draft in winter gives you a cold. Why? Because in the latter case you allowed God's pure air to manifest at a low level. In both instances it was nothing but pure ozone, filled with life and health, but it became to you just what you conceived it to be.

All things become new through the law of transmutation. Just as the clouds lift in the presence of the sun, revealing the rainbow, and the mountains behind them, so the Indwelling Power of Christ will transform every anxiety, fear and pain into a rainbow of peace, courage and health. The formidable problems of yesterday become the higher potencies of today. Corruption has put on incorruption, and man has become a universe unto himself.

MY FATHER'S BUSINESS

"Wist ye not that I must be about my Father's business?"

The Truth man cannot rest complacently upon his oars. He has work to do and tasks to accomplish. He has business with God. Until Simon met Christ his boat was the greatest thing in his life; it was his place of business, and his means of livelihood; nothing else mattered. Then came the call, "Follow me, and I will make you a fisher of men." Immediately Simon's boat took on a new meaning. Without a moment's hesitation he surrendered what he had. He gave up his business but did not quit it. Though there is every evidence that Simon was a religious man, like many today his religion was not vital. Fishing for fish was the live issue in his life. But a new Voice spoke and all was changed. The fish business became small and religion became large. Henceforth, Simon was Christ's and his property also was Christ's. There is a great lesson here, for before Christ came that way had Simon been asked, "Whose is that boat?" he would have answered,

"It is mine." Then Christ enters into Simon's thinking and the boat changes ownership. "It is Christ I care for," he says, "and I care for my boat for Christ." Along with Simon came his boat and the partnership was secure. Some of us are willing to give ourselves and others are willing to give their boats, but Christ demands our all. This is our "reasonable service," for unless ". . . He abide in the ship ye cannot be saved." If your business is to be the Father's Business, you must give Him not only yourself, but your boat as well.

Simon and those with him had fished all night anticipating taking their usual supply, but had caught nothing and naturally were disappointed. There were two sides to the boat, that of diversity and that of unity, and with that short-sightedness of the unenlightened they had selected the side of diversity, so their labor had been fruitless. Then Jesus appeared, and their spiritual eyes were opened. He told them to put out a bit farther and cast their nets on the other side (His side), and the catch was so great they could not haul it in. This is what always take place when we work in unity, in the consciousness of the One. "All things are ready," but it may be there is need to move to the other side of the boat. Let the Father direct your business and you cannot fail.

Christ, and right-thinking, are essential to every business, and nothing will so enhance your occupation as to dwell in the vision of the One. It makes no difference whether you are a plumber, a seamstress or a corporation lawyer, the state of your business will depend on the ownership of your boat. After all, the particular branch of business in which you happen to be has nothing to do with your success; it is the cosmic thinking you put into it that counts. "He who is fit can enter into the possession of all things." You will be successful in proportion to the right thought which you put into that you are doing. Bad weather, depression and failure are not "The Father's Business." Kill such thoughts at their inception, and row out a little farther into the Sea of Truth. Put Christ at the helm, and your nets will be full. All business is good business if Christ be in it. And all business will be prosperous if your mind is prosperous. There can be no confusion on the surface until there is confusion at the center.

MAN

Man is a tripartite being, and a distinct model of the universe manifesting as body, mind and spirit. The body is the sensitive vehicle of the soul, one in essence with matter. The soul (mind) is the subjective consciousness or reservoir of submerged power. The Spirit is the active principle of God in man, related to Truth. And the three are one—expressing as personality.

In the terrestrial body man is related to the finite, sense and materiality. In the soul (mind) he is related to intelligence and power. In the Spirit he is related to Cause, Wisdom and Infinity.

The Spirit in man is unlimited, and because of its mergence with the Universal Mind, is inexhaustible. This Mind is all-wise, all-intelligent, and contains the answer to every question and the solution to every problem. Being related to Cause through Spirit, man's unfoldment is eternal.

RECIPROCAL ACTION

Since there is a reciprocal action between the Mind of God and the mind of man, we can consciously draw upon this Divine. Power at will. Intelligent energy, however, is released through thought. Our thoughts are weak or strong, according to the amount of Universal Energy in them.

One can stand before a deaf man, blow into his ears and repeat the word "Ephphatha" and say, "Be thou opened," but it takes the consciousness of union with the Divine Power before the man's ears may be actually opened.

All words spoken for healing must be out lets of Universal Power. The human will can do nothing constructive or permanent. Working in God consciousness as Jesus did, you will say: "Not my will, but Thine be done." Success will always depend upon consciousness of a deep sense of corporate mental and Spiritual unity.

*   *   *   *   *

Here I take leave of you for the time. If I have been able to make plain, even partially, the elements of the subject, I am more than satisfied. It is a subject not easy of assimilation, because of the material distractions by which we all are confronted. "The wisdom of this world is foolishness with God," said Paul, realizing how vitally necessary it is to rise above human sagacity to place oneself en rapport with the Divine.

Therefore may I again urge upon those seeking to secure the blessing of communion with the Most High that they be not weary in well-doing, for the gratification which attends upon successful endeavor will surely be theirs if they faint not, but persevere and wait on the Lord!

Raisa - Mystic Alchemist

Energy Healing, Chakra Alignment, Sacred Geometry, Sound Healing

Tammy:
I was blessed with a healing session by Raisa last week. She felt like a friend and like-minded gentle soul with comforting Mother Mary essence pouring through her words. Raisa was so in-tuned to my blocks and traumas held within my field. She used her connection to ascended masters I've resonated with such as Yeshua, Mother Mary, Mary Magdalene, Lady Vesta & Amethyst and archangels Metatron, Michael and others to help clear these.

I was able to address childhood trauma situations to flip the stuck energy I've held onto over the years. She also picked up on a few traumatic past-life scenes that have affected my current life. I am an intuitive energy healer who truly felt the shift and healing within. I now feel so much lighter and have clarity regarding my path.

So much love and gratitude to you both, Raisa and Barry for presenting her to my world! (More Testimonials on following Pages)

Contact Raisa to book an Energy Healing
or Chakra Alignment session:
www.RaisinYourIsness.com
raisinyourisness@hotmail.com

Shannon:

This BEAUTIFUL sister...our Raisa... is a treasure beyond compare! After my experience in my personal session with Raisa... the ABSOLUTE confirmation I received, that could ONLY be confirmed by HER mind you... this session solidified EVERYTHING for me. I KNOW that this sister... she is a formidable, magnificent & IRREPLACEABLE component in this Earth plane story we all are invested in! IF YOU ARE DRAWN TO HER FOLLOW YOUR HEART

No other can do what SHE is gifted to do for YOU... YES YOU!

I LOVE YOU dear sister! I am forever grateful for what only you could do and DID for me! I would have happily paid any price for what you gave me! I URGE YOU ALL to schedule a session with this beloved one!

P.S. thank you Barry for sharing her with us all!

Natasha:

I would like to thank Barry for introducing us to Raisa. I have had 2 consultations with her in the last month and I am in total awe of what transpired. Raisa is such a beautiful caring soul! She connected with me as though she has known me forever. Her love and dedication in assisting others is so touching. I had an amazing experience and some profound healing. I received a message from Jeshua which brought tears to my eyes. I could feel the LOVE in the message that was given to me and I will remember and cherish His message forever. Raisa has really helped me in confronting fears, trauma and past life karma. I have found the reason for my skin problems which I never would have thought it'd be possible. It is amazing what guilt and shame from past lives can actually do to your body. Her healing and that from our Angelic beings has really made a huge difference in my life. I can feel it in my energy. Raisa has a lovely sense of humour, always reminding you not to take life and yourself so seriously. I really feel like a heavy weight has been lifted off my soul. Thank you so much! Much Love!

Ariel:

Raisa... Divine Raisa... You are a Treasure to this Life, and I thank All That Is, and this also Treasured YT channel for the priceless blessing which was our session this AM. Every moment of the session was a fractal explosion of wonderful intuitive & divinely guided perfection. I honor your sincere, caring, graceful, playful, soothing, encouraging, transformational, empowering, and so beautiful demonstration / embodiment of Goddess energy and presence. I am so honored & thankful to have been guided to You. To have invested in the patience, time, energy, and resources to share sacred healing and uplifting time with You. I will remember the session Always. And I will look forward to any and all ways our Creator deems it harmonious to connect again. I could go on and on and on, so please accept my parting acknowledgment of your blessing to this realm, my Heart & Spirt, my Life, and the Lives of all those who may be positively impacted via your assistance. Blessings, and Gratitude, a thousand times over and over again. Namaste... Namaste... Namaste...

B.G.

I have just finished a healing session with Raisa. The experience was remarkable! I am still buzzing! I heard about her from this channel, so thank you deeply Barry!

Raisa is so lovely to talk to, and intuitively guided, knows how to get to the hidden roots of our issues. She calls upon ascended masters, archangels and such to do deep energetic clearing and healing work. It was like being guided through the deep layers of myself, releasing the things that don't serve me and filling every cell with light. I purged, and I absorbed new energy, and came out feeling uplifted and renewed. Raisa helped me to find things in myself that I had been cut off from, and to heal wounds I had tried to bury. She has also given me helpful ideas to continue to improve things my life.

I am so blessed to have found Raisa, and ever grateful for the healing work she has done. She is as authentic as they come. Truly an earth angel! Thank you, thank you, thank you!

YouTube Channels of Interest:

Giving Voice to the Wisdom of the Ages

Over 5,000 audios, hundreds of
Spiritual and Metaphysical
audio books including
Robert A Russell, Dr Murdo MacDonald Bayne,
Napoleon Hill, Jeshua, Kryon and many more.

I AM Meditations and Affirmations

Hundreds of I AM Meditations,
Daily affirmations and more.

Raisin' Your Isness

Metaphysical Musings, Channelings,
Sound Healing Songs

Milton Keynes UK
Ingram Content Group UK Ltd.
UKHW041903021224
3259UKWH00001B/46